WELCOME!

This is your opportunity to become a real-life designer and have some high-fashion fun along the way.

The sections in this book – from seasonal collections and glamorous gowns, to up-to-date streetwear and essential accessories – give you a chance to explore your passion for fashion and experience the different disciplines of design. There is a section at the back filled with fabulous looks from the past and classic clothing from around the world to give you inspiration. When you are done doodling, you will be ready to present your unique collections on the catwalk and launch a global media campaign.

What are you waiting for? Grab your pen and get going ... the world of fashion awaits.

Sally

Editor

THE RED-CARPET COLLECTION

Viva la diva!

Design a diamond necklace that sparkles like the star you are.

Add divine detail to this sleek gown to take the red carpet by storm.

Floral frills and pretty prom queens.

Keep these pretty prom dresses looking young and fresh, with fun frills.

Good old-fashioned glamour.

Design some show-stopping shoes.

Cover the dress with sparkles and complete the train
for an award-winning look.

The Charity Ball calls ...

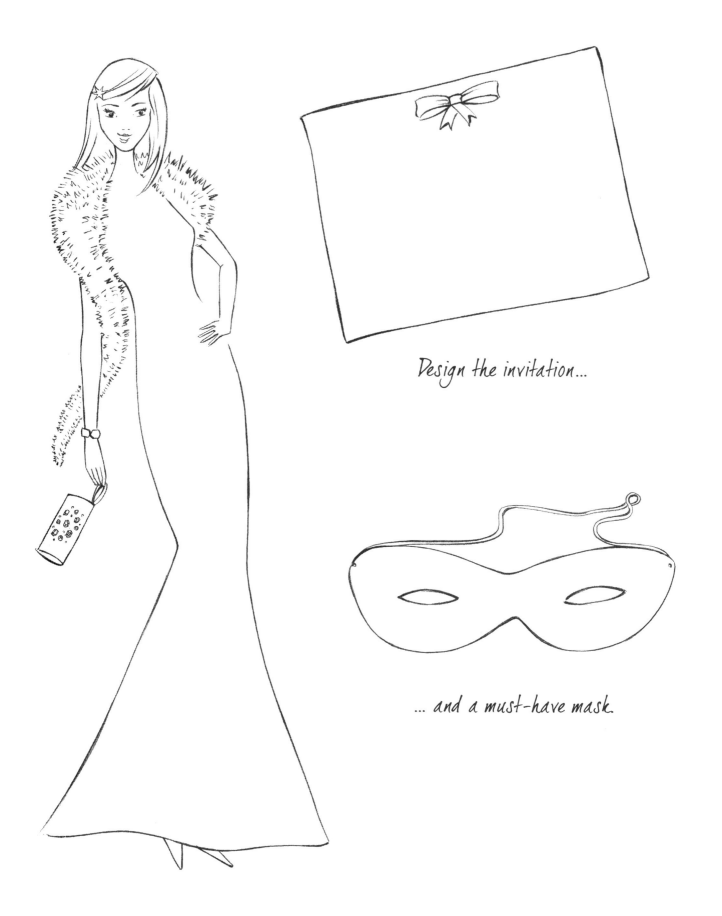

Design the invitation...

... and a must-have mask.

... for glamour for a good cause.

Finish these beautiful ball gowns.

Breathtaking bridesmaids ...

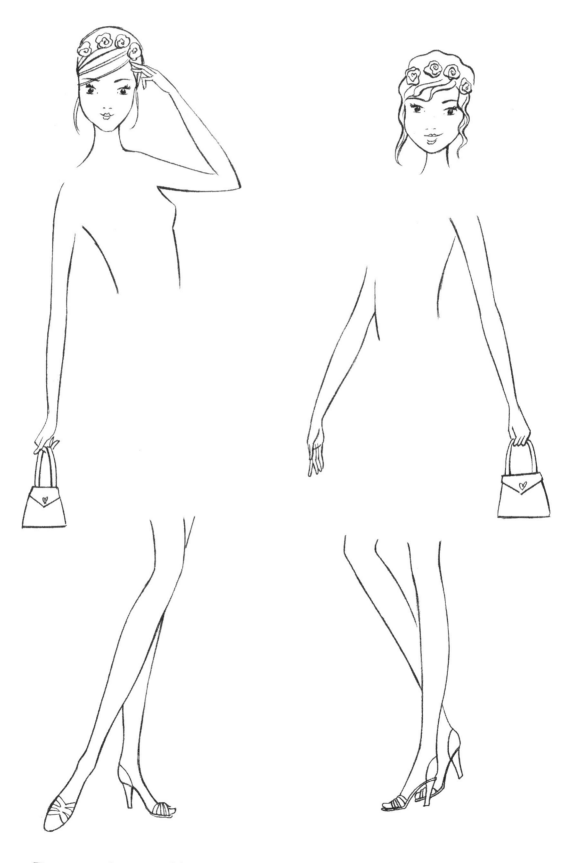

Design two different looks for the bridesmaids.

... to a beautiful bride.

Finish the tiara.

Draw the bouquet from above.

Design her wonderful wedding dress and bouquet.

The Christmas party.

Design a gorgeous handbag to go
with these festive dresses.

Give these dresses some Christmas sparkle.

And the award goes to ...

Finish these priceless
diamond earrings.

Give the movie star a gorgeous gown.

THE SPRING/SUMMER COLLECTION

April showers.

Draw a gorgeous pattern for the raincoats ...

... and one for the umbrellas.

Add a splash of colour to spring, with bright brollies
and wild Wellington boots.

Down on the farm.

Design a cool cowboy hat ...

... and some great boots.

Give these cowgirls some dungarees and decorate their cowboy boots.

Tea for two.

Design floral patterns for the
tea dresses.

Give the dresses some divine detail.

Keep classic cardigans cute.

Cover the cardigans in beautiful embroidery and beads.

A day at the races.

You need a hat to stay ahead.

Design hats to give their outfits some chapeau-chic.

Shorts and sweets.

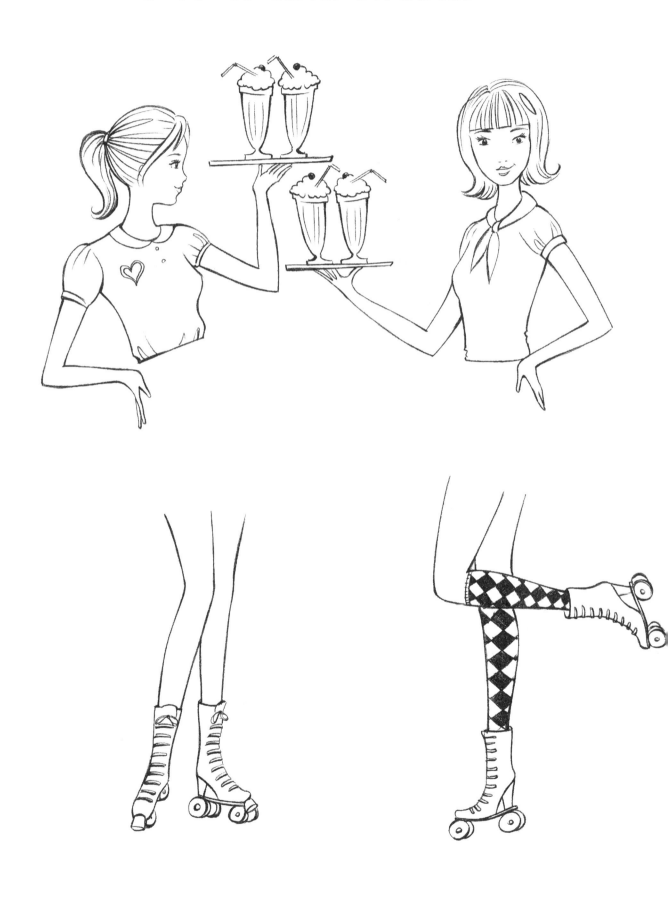

Sassy shorts are the perfect way to stay cool.

Design some super-hot hot pants.

Decorate the
shopping bags.

Summer in the city.

Design the outfit for this girly getaway.

Ship ahoy!

Give these sassy seafaring gals bold buttons
and nautical stripes.

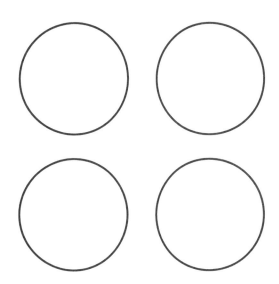

Design some buttons with a nautical theme. Detail is everything.

It's a jungle out there.

Gear up for summer with some super safari clothes. Give these girls cool combats, short-sleeved shirts and sunhats.

The temperature is rising ...

Skirts may be short, but accessories are big news.

... and so are the hemlines.

Team sassy skirts with bright bags, belts, sunhats and shades.

It's a shore thing.

Come up with a cute beach cover-up.

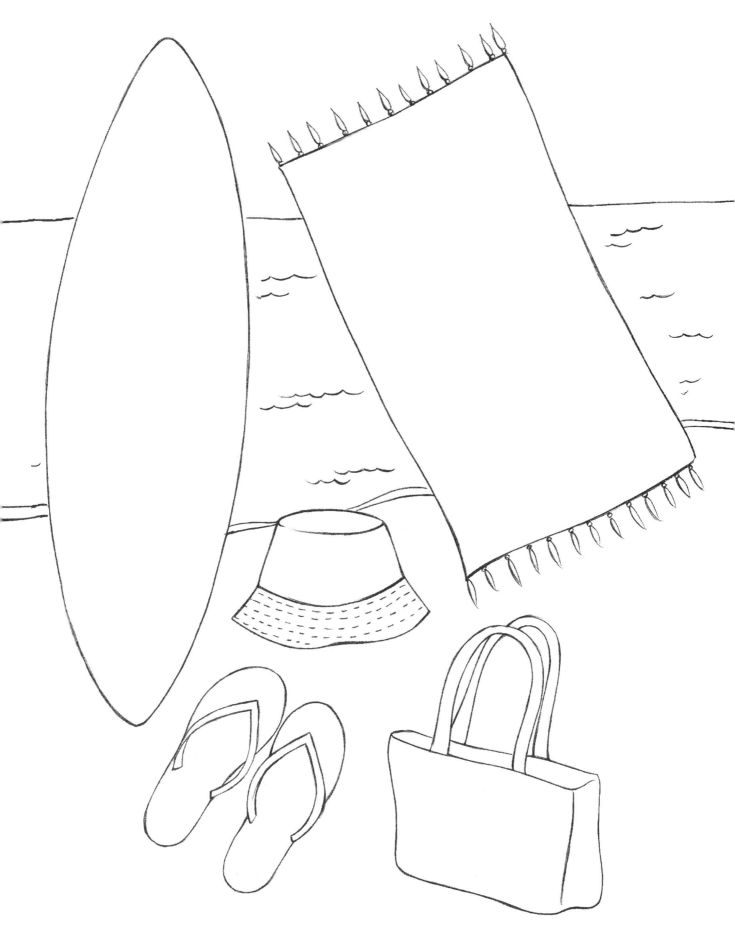

Set out into the sun in style with your own range of beach accessories.

Damsels of the deep.

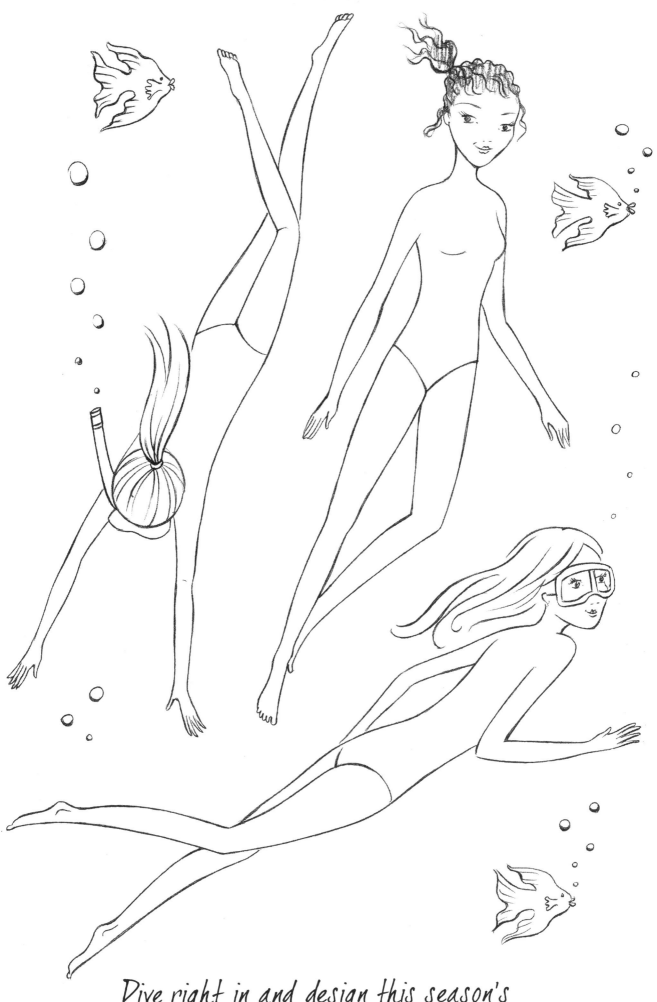

Dive right in and design this season's
brilliant bathing suits and bikinis.

Short trousers in – ankles out.

Design some cute calf-length trousers.

Marvellous flip-flops.

Design some fun and fancy flip-flops.

So right, sarong.

Create a seashell pattern and
then decorate the sarong.

THE AUTUMN/WINTER COLLECTION

Nights are drawing in.

Design a bright pattern for
the bag and one for the coat

Brighten up autumn days with a patterned coat
and contrasting bag.

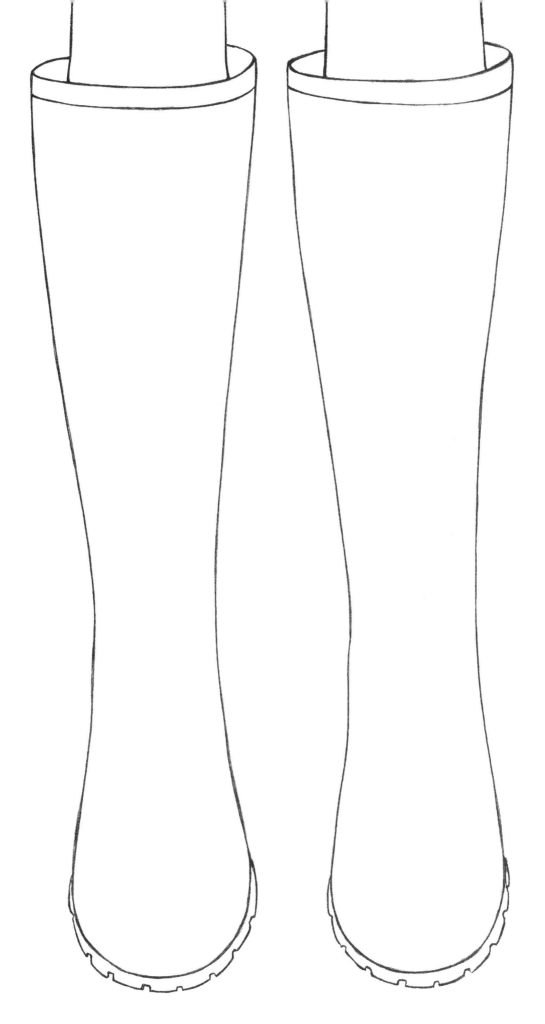

Add the perfect pair of printed boots to complete the look.

Up to your knees in style.

This season's boots are knee-high.

Design a collection of must-have boots.

It's hip to be square.

Give these geek-chic girls pretty pleated skirts and tops.

Packing a poncho.

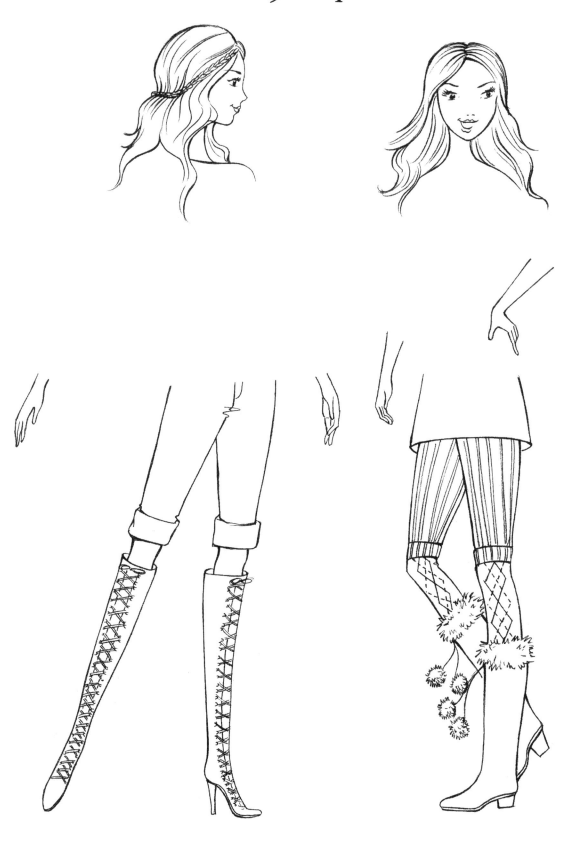

Sleeves are so last season. Pep up these ponchos with punchy patterns.

Woollies are essential this winter.

Give these girls some woolly jumpers, hats and scarves.

Check them out.

Cover their outfits in tartans and checks.

City slickers.

Make these models look like they mean business
in sharp suits.

Top coats.

Finish these winter coats with some stylish buttons and lapels.

Fur is fine, as long as it's fake.

Finish these fabulous fake-fur jackets and coats.

Sweet sweaters.

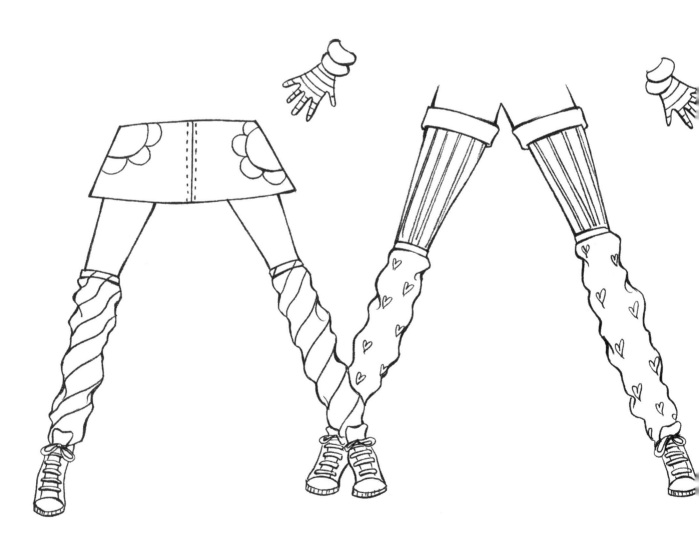

Give these girls some cosy jumpers.

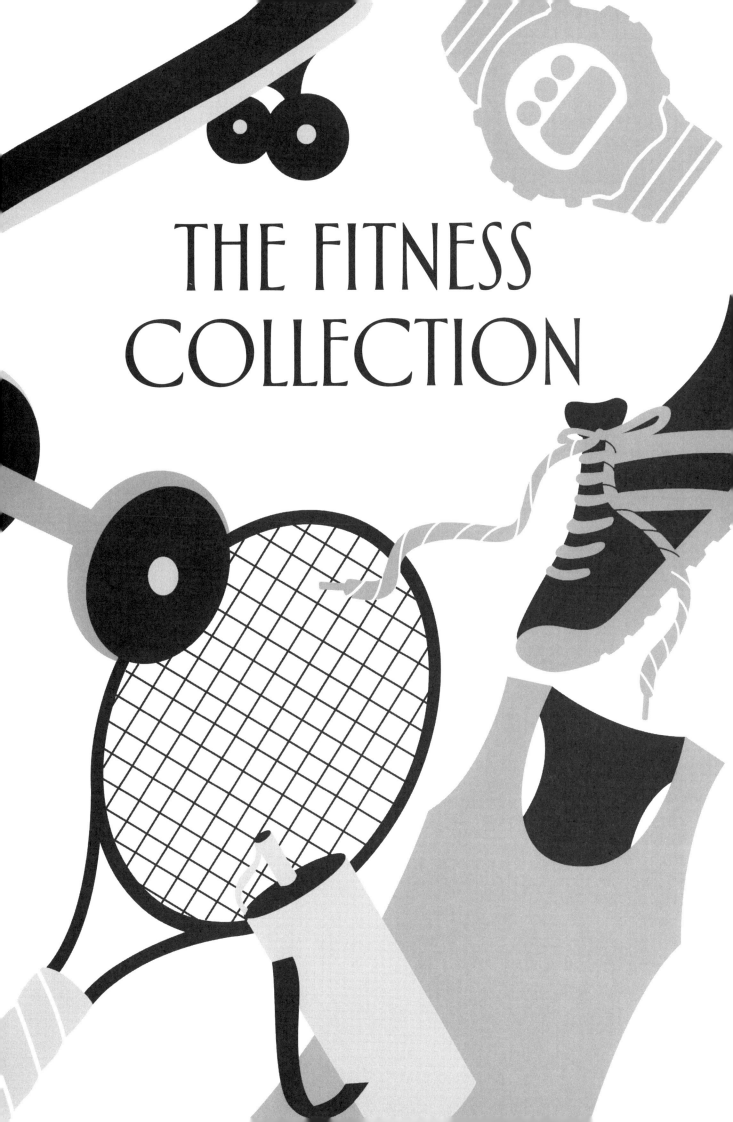

THE FITNESS COLLECTION

Hit the slopes in style.

Design their ski jackets and winter boots.

Get fit to be seen.

Be fit and fabulous by designing your own range of gym-wear.

Green with envy.

Tee off in style with some gorgeous golf-wear ...

... and a groovy golf bag.

Saddle up in style.

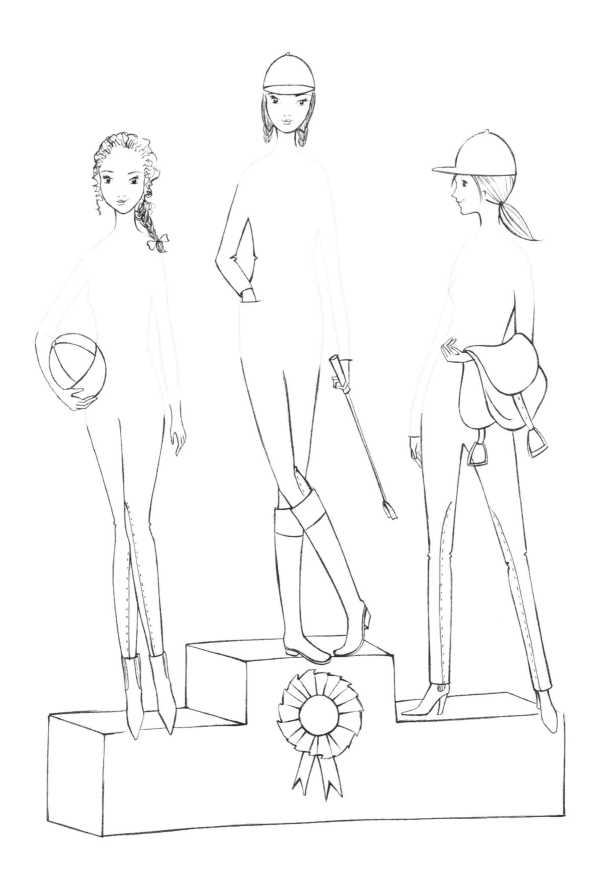

Design a collection of riding gear and decorate the saddle.

Game, set and matching.

Give this designer doubles team desirable tennis whites.

Better skate than never.

Give these girls some super-stylish skater clothes
and decorate their boards.

Give us an 'S', give us a 'T', give us a 'Y-L-E'.

Give these cheerleaders some uniforms to shout about

To cap it all ...

Create a cap for the baseball player.

STREET
STYLE

Punk it up.

Give these punk princesses ripped T-shirts.

Sneakin' around.

Give these girls some sassy sneakers.

Bohemian rhapsody!

Team floaty skirts with gypsy jewels.

Ad-hoc frock.

Create the main pattern
for the fabric.

Add an 'accent' pattern
for the sleeves.

Mix the bold patterns you've created for that
thrown-together look.

Badges of honour.

Make a statement - cover the lapels with designer badges.

What statement do you want to make?

Design some badges and then cover the jacket.

Born to ride.

The leather look is hot, on or off the road.

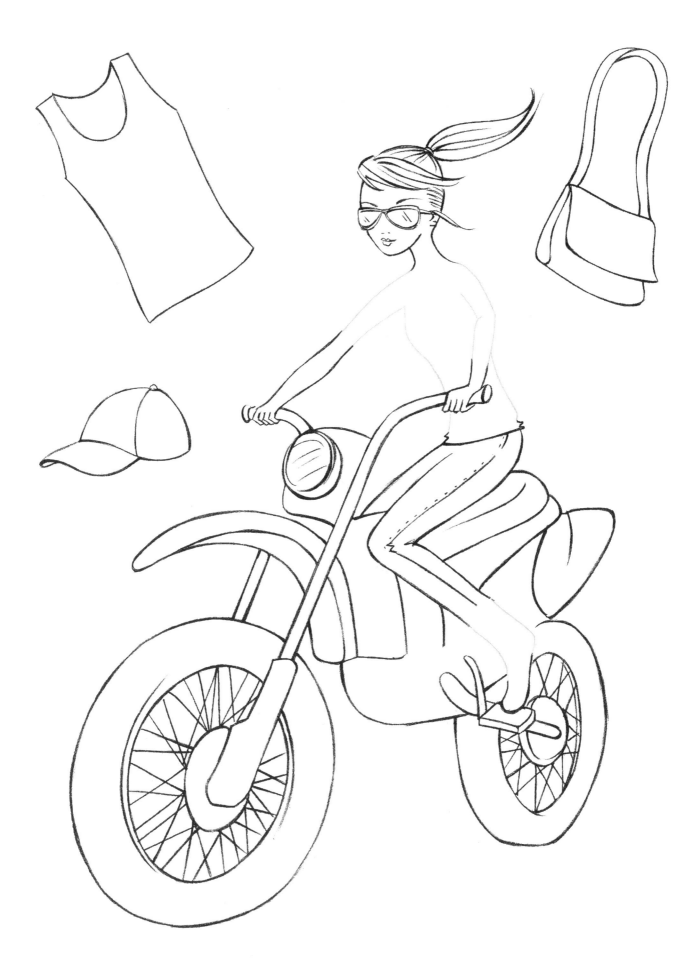

Give these biker babes some biker jackets and boots.
Don't forget to decorate the bike.

Rock-chick chic.

Rock and roll is never out of style. Make her outfit super cool with a band T-shirt and distressed jeans.

A bit of military magic.

Design your own camouflage and then cover her combat clothes.

Decorate this shirt, too.

Psychedelic patterns.

Cover the dress in this super
psychedelic pattern.

Neon brights and disco lights.

Design some perfect
platform shoes.

Grab your shades, you'll need them to see this season's designs.

Hitting the decks.

Decorate the DJ's dress for the disco.

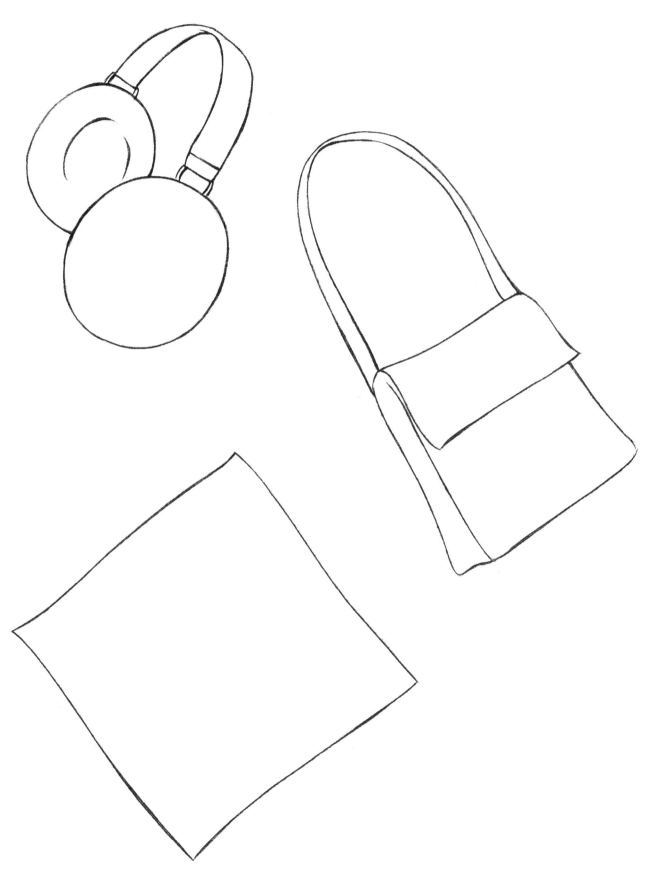

Style her accessories and records to go with her look

Get the party in full swing.

Team terrific tassels with far-out fringing.

ESSENTIAL ACCESSORIES

The ultimate party shoes.

Put the soul back into these party shoes.

Bring on the ballet pump.

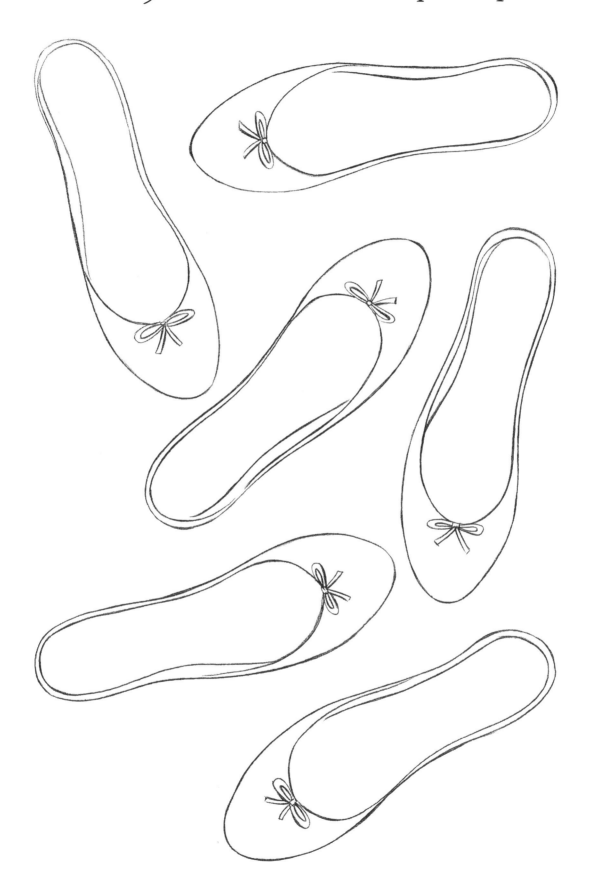

Put your best foot forward with this season's patterned pumps.

Design some terrific tights.

Lace up these sandals.

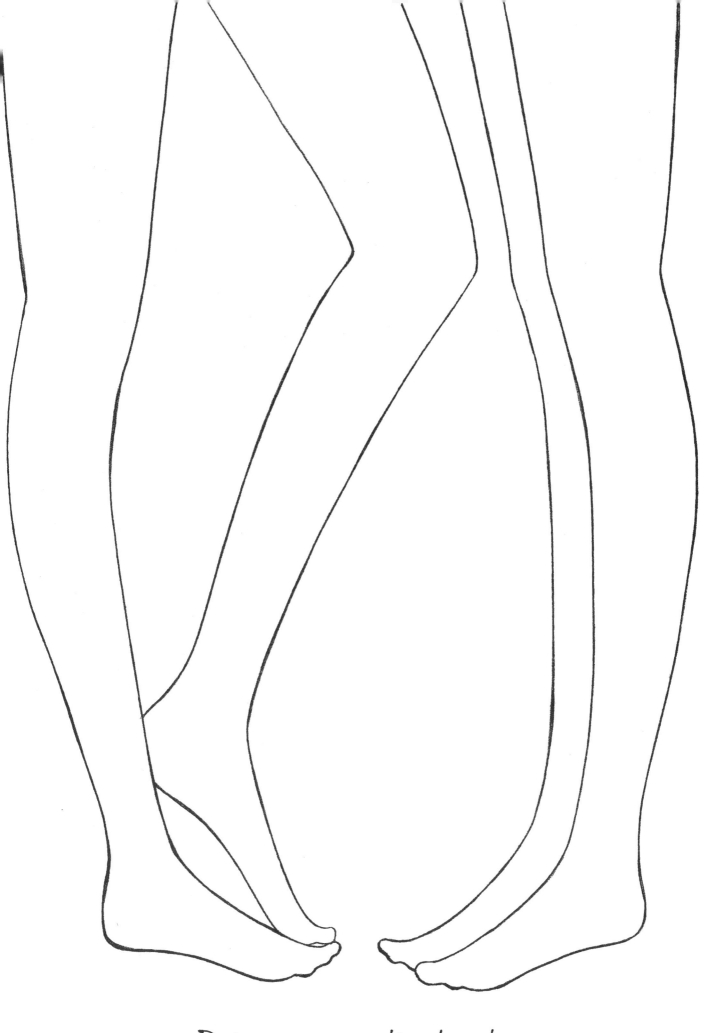

Design some sensational socks.

Get carried away ...

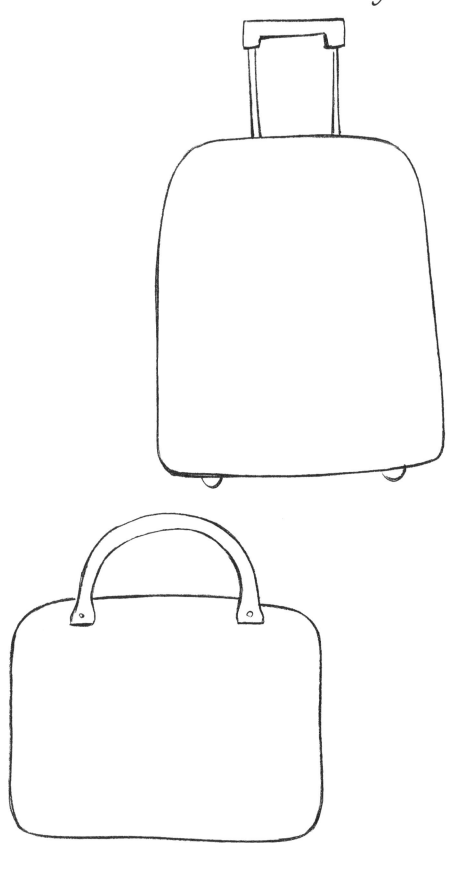

Make this baggage bright and beautiful.

... with this season's luggage collection.

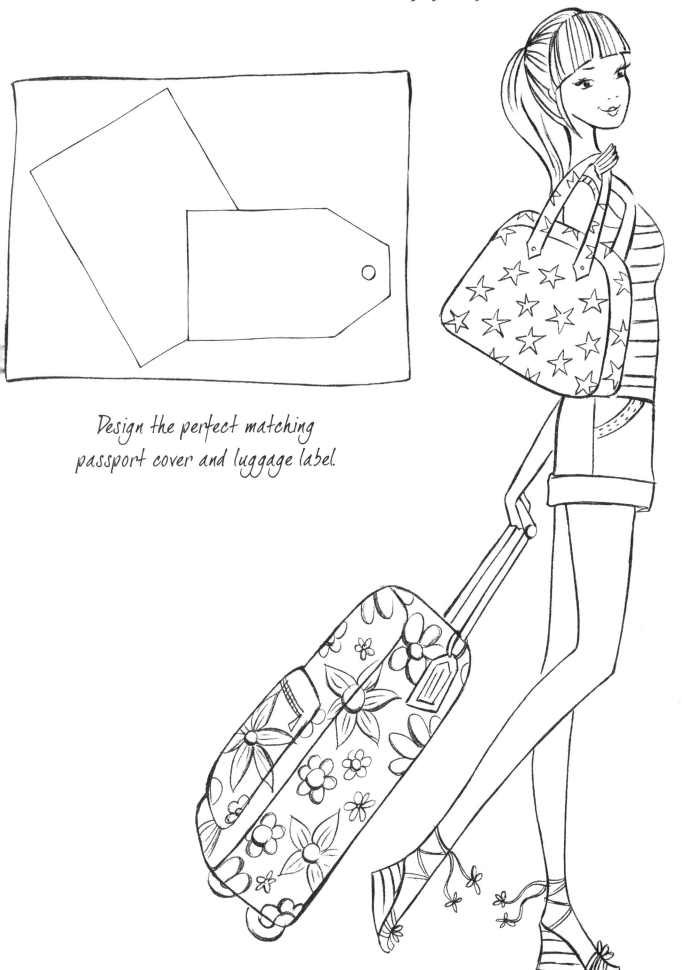

Design the perfect matching
passport cover and luggage label.

Must-have handbags.

Finish these fabulous handbags.

A bag to keep hold of.

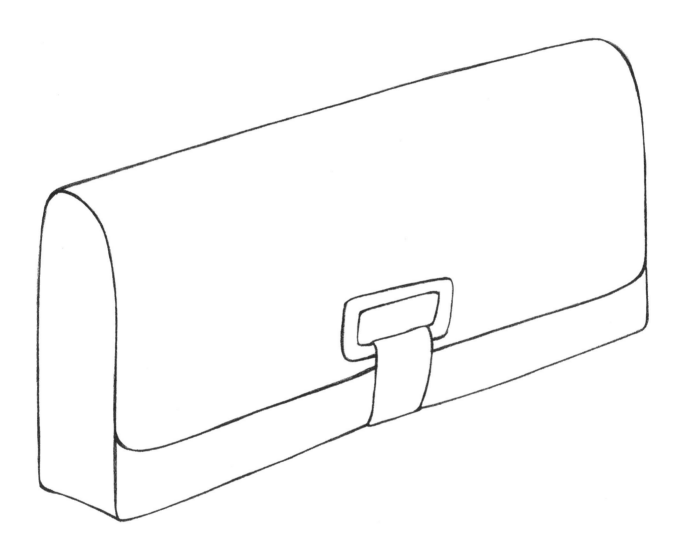

Make this clutch bag beautiful with beading.

And that's a wrap.

Design a collection of pretty scarves and pashminas.

Finish their outfits by adding detail to their wraps.

Bold bandanas.

Keep hair under control with these happening headscarves.
Finish the scarves and give them pretty patterns.

Funky watches.

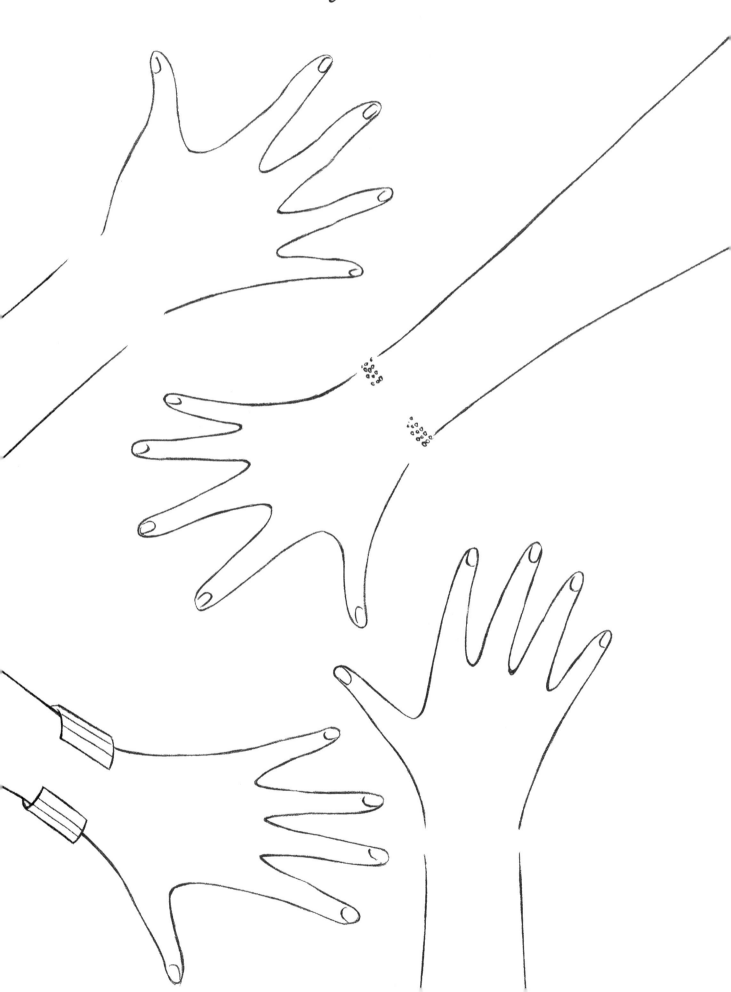

Charmed.

Fill the bracelet with charms.

Desirable jewellery.

Design your own range of earrings.

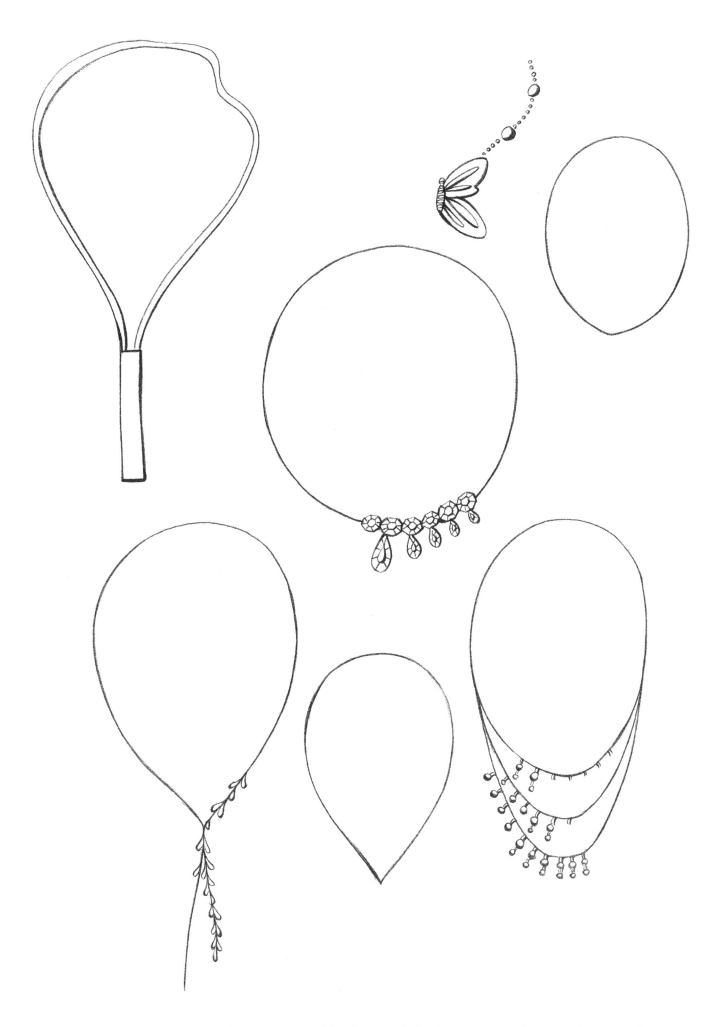

Finish these necklaces with beautiful pendants and beads.

Purrr-fect pet-wear.

Give these cool cats and precious pooches some style.

Cool shades.

Get a grip.

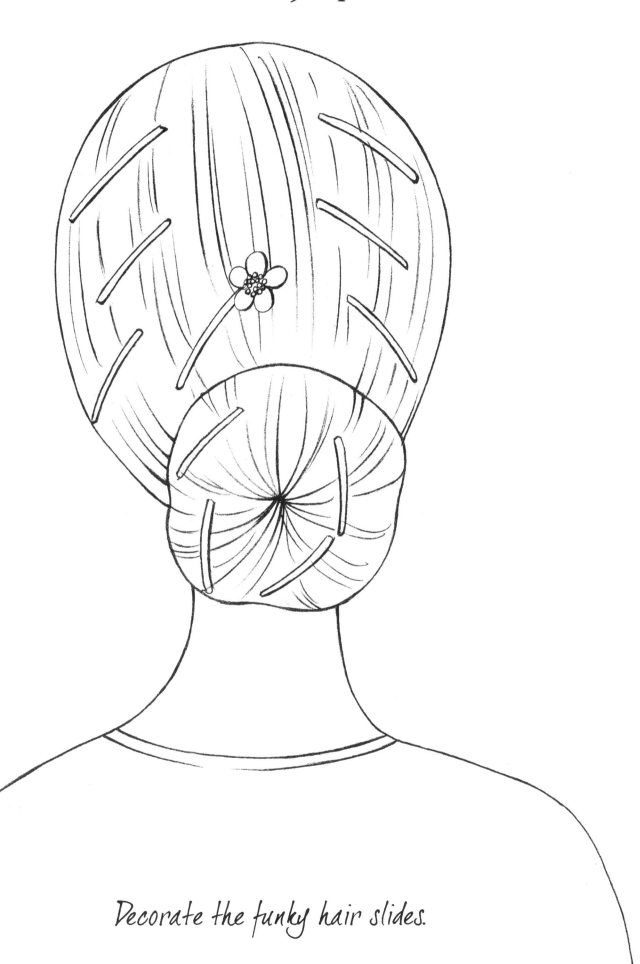

Decorate the funky hair slides.

Sleep tight.

Decorate her beautiful eye mask ...

... and her gorgeous pyjamas.

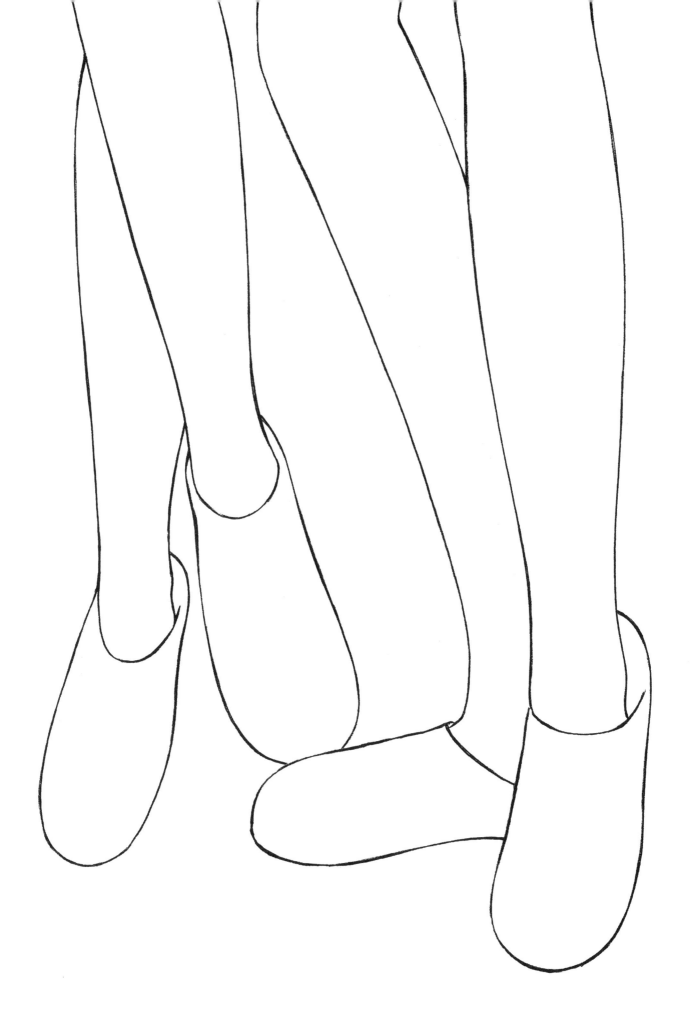

Decorate their comfy slippers.

FASHION
BUSINESS

From fine ... to fabulous.

Give the model a designer makeover.

It's show time.

Give the model dramatic catwalk make-up and hair.

Backstage at the fashion show.

Draw your own collection of catwalk clothes on the rail.

Finishing touches.

Get these models ready to take to the catwalk.

Make the finishing touches to their glamorous gowns.

Bangles and rings.

Draw the final outfit of the show.

Front-row seats.

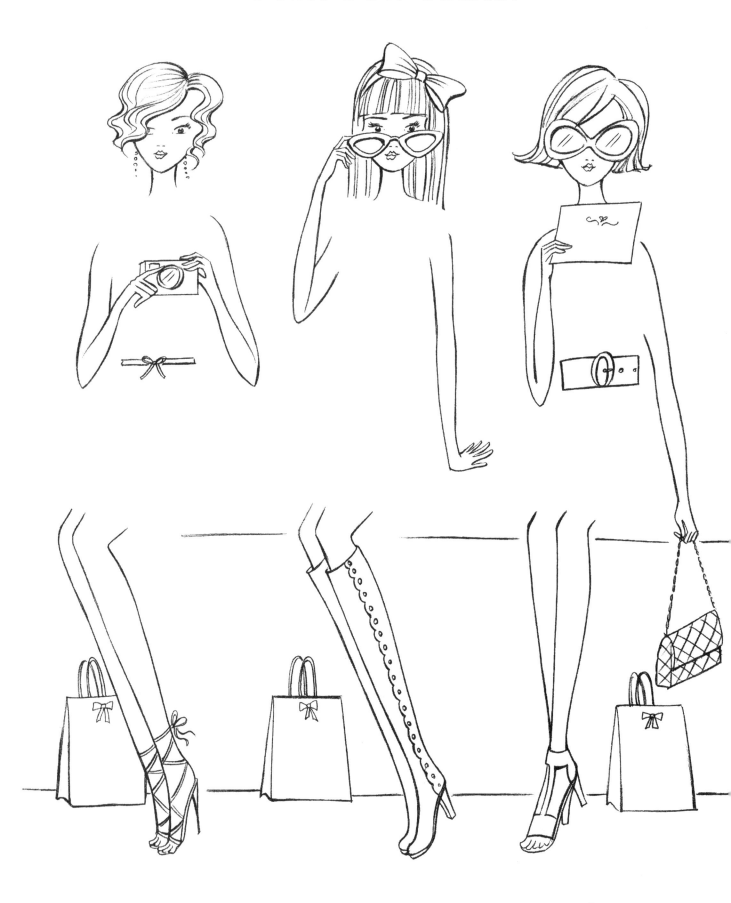

What are they wearing on the front row of the fashion show?

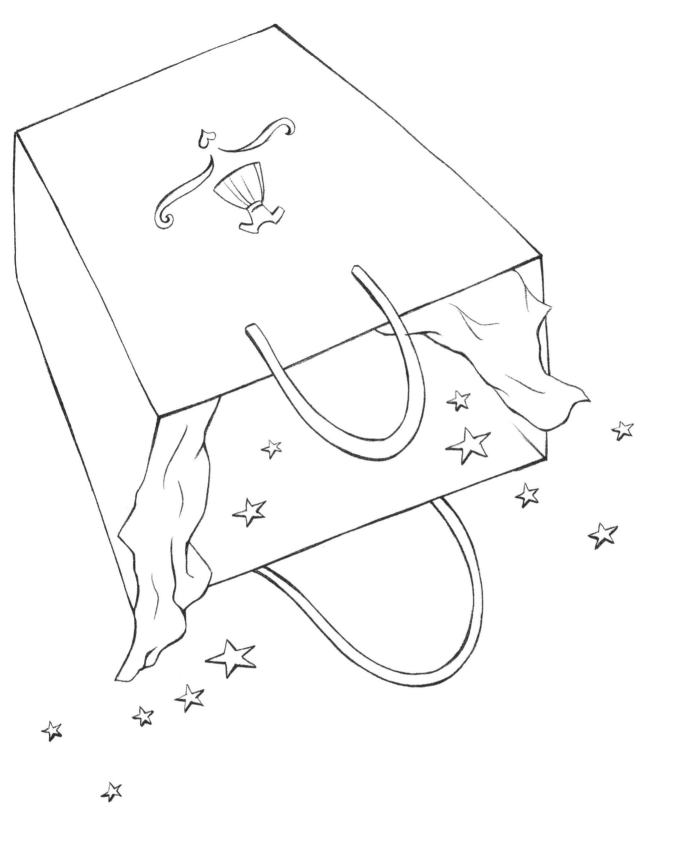

What's in the after-show party bag?

What's on the front cover of the fashion magazine?

Your designer fragrance.

Design the bottle.

Advertise your designer fragrance on the billboard.

Girls just want to have fun.

Style the girl band so they can be top of the fashion charts.

Catwalk style.

Draw your collection on the runway models.

Kiss and make-up.

Design your own range of beauty products ...

... with the prettiest packaging.

For the boys?

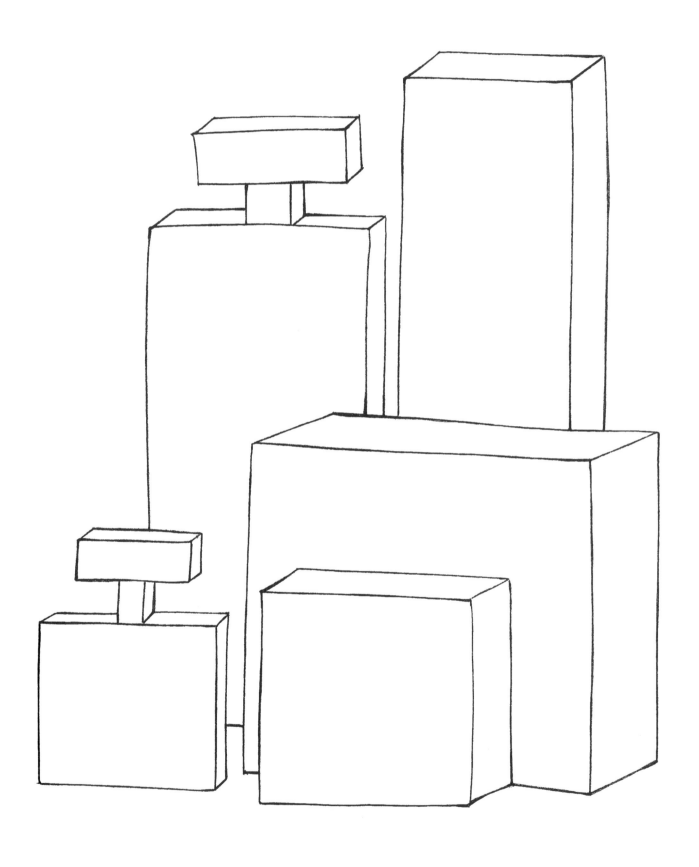

Design a product range for men.

Apply your beauty products.

Add some nail varnish.

Skinny or flared for your designer denims?

On-trend T's.

Use bold letters to design your own range of signature T-shirts.

Draw the clothes in your shop window.

Your designer home.

Design your ideal home.

Your designer wardrobe.

Organize your designer clothes in the wardrobe.

GET INSPIRED

Mighty Aphrodites.

Give these goddesses beautiful brooches.

Wink like an Egyptian.

Give the model make-up like Cleopatra.

Gorgeous geisha chic.

Design a pattern for her kimono ...

... and one for her belt

Flowing flamenco frills.

Finish her skirt with ruffles.

Heroines from history.

Finish their dresses with rich embroidery.

In a flap.

Give the dancers dresses from the 1920s.

Chic checks and hot spots.

Finish their fabulous 1950s frocks with
hip and happening polka dots.

Swing out sisters.

Get into the swing of the 1960s with bright geometric patterns.

Flower-power fabulous.

Finish their far-out fashions.

Curtain call.

Dress these dancers in delicate designs.